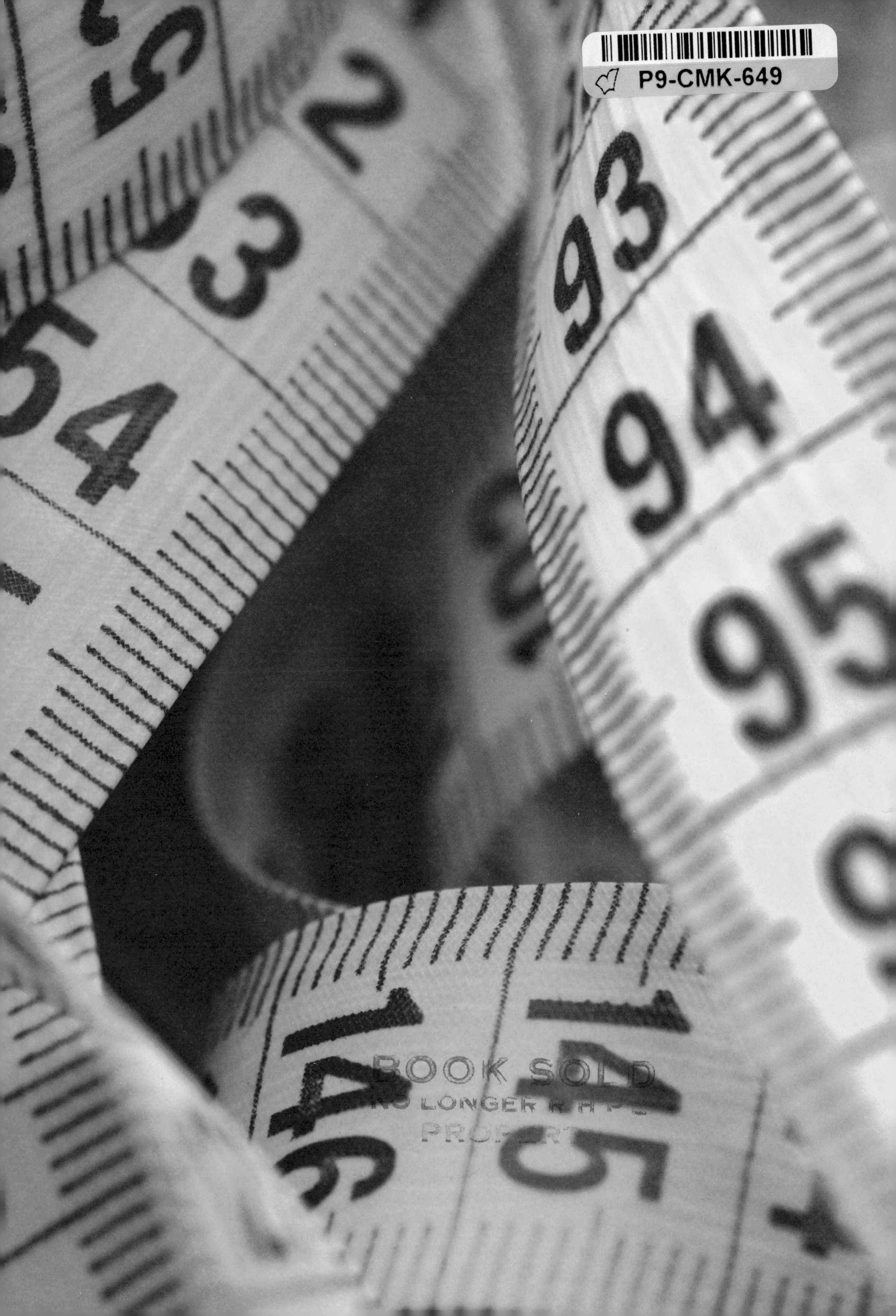

GET THE MEASURE

Units and Measurements

Rob Colson

Children's Press®
An Imprint of Scholastic Inc.

Acknowledgments and Photo Credits

Library of Congress Cataloging-in-Publication Data
A CIP catalog record for this book is available from the Library of Congress.

Copyright © The Watts Publishing Group, 2016
First published by Franklin Watts 2016
Published in the United States by Scholastic Inc. 2018

Printed in China

SCHOLASTIC, CHILDREN'S PRESS, and associated logos are trademarks and/or registered trademarks of Scholastic Inc.

1 2 3 4 5 6 7 8 9 10 R 27 26 25 24 23 22 21 20 19 18

Photo Credits:
t-top, b-bottom, l-left, r-right, c-center, front cover-fc, back cover-bc
All images courtesy of Dreamstime.com unless indicated:
Inside front Professor25; fc, bc Pablo631; fcbl Markbeckwith; fctc Radub85; fctr, 25b dial-a-view/iStockphoto; 1c, 17t Supsup; 4l Gekaskr; 4l Ekaterina Nikolaenko; 4b Justk8; 5c Hjalmeida; 5cb Koszivu; 6c, 28tl Johan63; 7b, 16bc, 29tc Msanca; 8b, 30bl Mzwonko; 9 NASA; 9c, 17c Mexrix; fccb, 10l Hamster3d; 10c, 22br, 31tr Macrovector; bcc, 11t Tverdohlib; 11b NASA; 12t Frameangel; fcbl, 12c Mrallen; 12b Experimental; 13b Filipefrazao84; 15c NASA; 15b Blakeley; 16t Zaclurs; 16tr Roberto Giovannini; 16bl Dragon_27; 16bc Shaeree Mukherjee; 16br Bokicai; 17c Fallsview; 17bl, 29tr Insima; 17c Ciro Amedeo Orabona; 17br Red33; 18t Mrmarshall; 18c Luke Thomas/ Shutterstock, Inc.; 18b Nicolasprimola; fctl, 19t Rudall30; 19b Red Orbit; bctr, 20b Cory Thoman; fcbr, 21t, 29br Forplayday; fcbr, 21t, 29br Dundanim/Shutterstock.com; 21b, 28tr NASA; bctc, 22t Zinchik; 23tr Leo Blanchette; 23bl Nicolas Fernandez; 23bc Dannyphoto80; 23bc Jehsomwang; 23br Topgeek; 24b Razvan Ionut Dragomirescu; 24t Vectorlibellule; 25c Pppfoto15; 26l Onairjiw; 27t Roman Yatsyna; 27c Haiyin; 27b Rasà Messina Francesca; fctc, 28b drmakkoy/iStockphoto.com; 30tc Tuulijumala; 30br Milosluz; 32t Stylephotographs

Teaching Guide ⇢

Visit this Scholastic Web site to download the Teaching Guide for this series:
www.factsfornow.scholastic.com
Enter the keywords **Get the Measure**

A History of Measuring

When people first moved into towns and cities thousands of years ago, they needed systems of measurement. These allowed them to build homes, make clothes and tools, and trade with each other.

1 cubit

The earliest known standard measurement is the cubit from ancient Egypt. It is based on the length from the end of the fingers to the elbow.

Rule of Thumb

"Rule of thumb" is a phrase that means a rough estimate of a measurement. Carpenters used to use their thumbs rather than rulers to measure their work. In many languages, the word for "inch" also means "thumb."

In some countries, horses are measured using hands. One hand equals 4 inches. The height of a horse is measured from the ground to its withers. Thoroughbred horses used for racing are about 16 hands high.

Body Measures

The imperial system of measurement (also called the customary or the English system) was devised for the British Empire in the 19th century. It has many lengths based on parts of the body. The U.S. still uses this system of measurement, but most other countries have switched to the metric system.

1 inch
about 2.5 cm. This is about the width of a thumb.

1 foot = 12 inches
about 30 cm. This is about the length of a foot.

1 hand = 4 inches
about 10 cm. This is about the width of a hand.

1 yard = 3 feet
about 90 cm. This is about the length of a stride.

Approx. 4 in

Approx. 1 ft

Going Metric

Today's standard international units of measurement, known as the metric system, were devised in revolutionary France more than 200 years ago.

In the 18th century, there were thousands of different units of measurement, and each town or area had its own system. In 1791, following the Revolution, the French decided to create one standard for all, based on multiples of ten. The measures are all derived from the standard length of **1 meter** (see page 6) and include measures of weight and volume.

Length and Distance

The metric unit of length is the meter. It was defined in 1793 by the French Academy of Sciences as one-ten-millionth of the distance on Earth's surface from the equator to the North or South Pole.

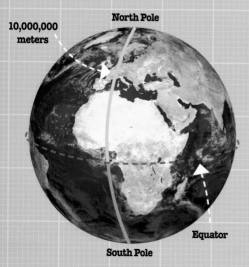

10,000,000 meters

North Pole

Equator

South Pole

3.5 m
3.5 m
3.5 m
3.5 m
3.5 m
3.5 m
3.5 m

200 meters starting line

The starting lines for the 200-meter race are staggered at half the distance of the 400-meter. This is because the athletes are running around only one bend, not two.

Today, the meter is defined exactly as the distance traveled by light in $1/299{,}792{,}458$ of a second.

Smaller distances start in millimeters, which can then be converted into centimeters and then meters.

1,000 mm = 100 cm = 1 m

Longer distances are often described in kilometers.

1 km = 1,000 m

The U.S. still uses the mile, an English unit of measurement, to describe distances.

1 mile = 1.609344 km

Leagues

In the Middle Ages (5th to 15th centuries), a common way to describe longer distances was the league. This was the distance a person could walk in an hour, which was roughly 3 miles, or 5 kilometers. People without horses would sometimes walk several days at a time to get from one town to another. If a town was 30 leagues away, a person needed to allow 30 hours to walk there.

"I think I'll stick to the 100-meter next time!"

Ready, Set, Go!

One lap of a running track is 400 meters, but that's only if you run on the inside lane. A full lap in the outside lane is about 450 meters. When athletes compete in a 400-meter race, their starting points are staggered so they all run the same distance.

Inside lane

400 meters starting line

Start lane 1

Start lane 2

Start lane 3

Start lane 4

Start lane 5

Start lane 6

Start lane 7

Start lane 8

7m 7m 7m 7m 7m 7m 7m

FINISH

Huge Distances

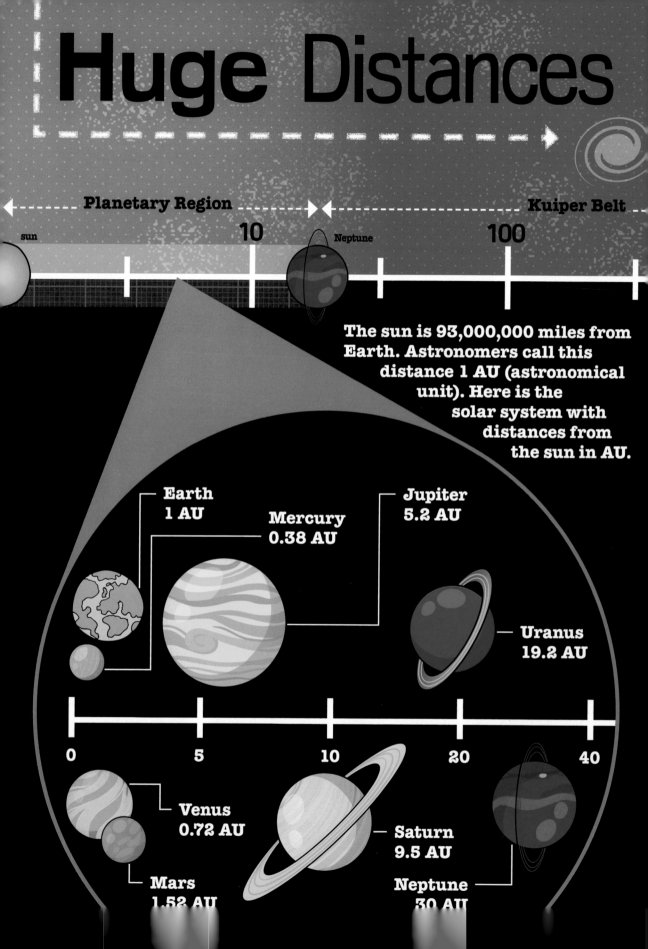

Planetary Region

Kuiper Belt

sun

10

Neptune

100

The sun is 93,000,000 miles from Earth. Astronomers call this distance 1 AU (astronomical unit). Here is the solar system with distances from the sun in AU.

Earth
1 AU

Mercury
0.38 AU

Jupiter
5.2 AU

Uranus
19.2 AU

0   5   10   20   40

Venus
0.72 AU

Saturn
9.5 AU

Mars
1.52 AU

Neptune
30 AU

Light-Year

To measure the enormous distances between stars, astronomers use a unit called a light-year. This is equal to the distance traveled in one year by light, the fastest thing in the universe.

1 light-year (ly) = 5.9 trillion miles

That's **5,900,000,000,000 mi**

1 ly = 60,000 AU

The nearest star to Earth after the sun is Alpha Centauri. **It is 4.4 ly** away, meaning that it is 264,000 times as far away from Earth as the sun is.

Alpha Centauri

Andromeda galaxy

MACS0647-JD

Our solar system is part of the Milky Way galaxy. This is a disk of stars **1,000 ly thick** and **100,000 ly across**. The nearest galaxy to the Milky Way is **Andromeda**. It is **2.5 million ly** from Earth.

The farthest galaxy we have spotted is **MACS0647-JD**, which is **13.3 billion ly** away. That means that the light that we are seeing now left the galaxy 13.3 billion years ago. We are seeing MACS0647-JD as it was a very long time ago—before Earth even existed.

Tiny
Distances

The smallest life-forms, bacteria, are just a few microns across.

1 micron (μm) = 1 millionth of a meter

The molecules that code for life, **DNA**, are about 2 nanometers (nm) across. These molecules are made of long chains of smaller molecules that are tightly coiled up. If DNA molecules were stretched out straight, they would be several centimeters long.

1 nanometer (nm) = 1 billionth of a meter

A hydrogen atom is about 25 picometers (pm) across.

1 picometer (pm) = 1 trillionth of a meter

Beard-Second

Not content with the standard measurements, physics students in the U.S. invented a measurement of their own.

The beard-second is a humorous unit of length inspired by the light-year but used for very short distances. There is some dispute as to how far that really is, but it's normally accepted to be 5 nanometers. That's

0.000000005 meter.

"Slow down, I'm growing faster than a beard-second!"

The Shortest Length Possible

Physicists calculate that there is a minimum length that cannot be divided up. This is called the Planck length, and it is about

10^{-35} meter, or $1/10^{35}$ meter.

The smallest thing we can see with the naked eye is a dot about 0.1 millimeter across: ⟶ ▢ If that dot were blown up to the size of the entire universe, a dot inside the dot that is 1 Planck length across would appear to be about **0.1 millimeter across**.

Nanotechnology

Nanotechnologists develop tiny machines out of individual molecules. They make motors, switches, gears, and pumps just a few hundred nanometers across. These miniature machines could be used by doctors to deliver medicine around the body.

In 2011, scientists made the first-ever molecule-sized motor, just 1 nanometer across.

These highly magnified nanogears are made from carbon nanotubes with benzene molecules attached on the outside to form interlocking "teeth."

11

Area

Area is a measure of the amount of surface a two-dimensional shape covers. The basic unit of area is the square yard, yd², which is the area of a square with sides one yard long.

A large umbrella has an area of about 1 yd².

Squaring a Yard

There are 36 inches in a yard. This means that on each side of a square yard there are 36 inches:

$$1 \text{ yd}^2 = 36 \times 36 = 1{,}296 \text{ in}^2.$$

Measuring Land

In the U.S., land area is measured in acres.

1 acre = 4,840 yd²

The acre was established in medieval times as the amount of land that could be plowed using a pair of oxen in one day.

The Hectare

In the metric system, land area is measured in hectares.

1 hectare = 10,000 m²

It is a little larger than a soccer field.

1 acre

1 hectare

The Amazon rain forest in South America covers an area of **2.1 million square miles**. During the 1990s, up to 11,580 square miles of forest were lost each year as people cleared the trees for farmland. That's an area the size of Belgium every year.

size of Belgium

20% of the Amazon rain forest has been lost in the past 40 years.

Governments have made efforts to slow down the forest clearing, and now only about **3,860 square miles** are being lost each year.

Volume

A liter is the volume of a cube with 10-cm sides.

1l = 10 cm x 10 cm x 10 cm = 1,000 cm³

There are 1,000 liters in 1 m³.

1 m

1 m

1 m

1 liter

10 cm

1 cm³

1 foot

1 acre-foot

66 feet

660 feet

In the U.S., large quantities of water in reservoirs or rivers are measured using a unit called the acre-foot. This is the volume of water that would cover an area of one acre to a depth of one foot.

1 acre-foot = just over 1,233 m³

Shipping Volume

Freight is carried around the world in container ships. Container size is measured using a unit called the **TEU**. TEU stands for

Twenty-Foot Equivalent Unit

Containers that are 1 TEU big are

20 feet (6.1 meters) long.

Their ends are squares with 8-ft (2.4-m) sides. Containers are a standard size so they can be stacked next to one another. Most containers are 40 ft (12.2 m) long, making them 2 TEU big. This is a good size to be transported by a truck once the container has been unloaded from the ship.

Olympic-Sized Swimming Pool

A standard Olympic swimming pool contains

2.5 million liters of water.

That's 660,430 gallons of water! That much water would keep an average household going for 10 years.

2 m

50 m

25 m

Astronomers measure volume in space in

cubic light-years.

Our Milky Way galaxy has a volume of about 8 trillion cubic light-years.

"I'm two TEU. What are you?"

Speed and Velocity

Speed is a measure of the distance traveled per unit of time. It is commonly measured in feet per second (f/s) or miles per hour (mph). An object's velocity is its speed in a particular direction.

The force of gravity causes objects to accelerate toward the center of Earth. The rate of acceleration is

32 f/s².

Acceleration

A change in an object's velocity by a force is called **acceleration**.

A change in speed caused by acceleration is measured in **feet per second per second**, or **f/s²**.

In Orbit
A satellite orbits at a constant speed, but it is also accelerating! The force of gravity affects its velocity by changing its direction to keep it in orbit.

Direction satellite would move without gravity

Gravity pulls satellite into circular orbit

Pull of gravity

Earth

Earth's gravity constantly pulls the satellite to stop it from flying off. In much the same way, if you swing a yo-yo above your head, the string pulls it toward you.

Top Speeds

Snail
3 f/h

Tortoise
5 mph

Human
28 mph

Racehorse
43 mph

Light Speed

Light travels at **186,272** miles per second. Nothing can move faster than the speed of light, which physicist Albert Einstein (1879–1955) described as the speed limit of the universe.

Thunder and Lightning

The speed of sound through air is 1,126 f/s. The difference between the **speed of sound** and the **speed of light** is the reason we hear thunder after we see lightning. The light reaches us almost instantly, but the sound may take many seconds. To work out how far away a lightning strike was, **count the seconds** between **seeing the lightning** and hearing the thunder. **Every five seconds represents one mile.**

**Cheetah
62 mph**

**Sailfish
68 mph**

**Fighter jet
2,174 mph**

Weight and Mass

When we talk about how much something weighs, we are usually referring to its mass, which is a measure of how much matter the thing contains.

Weight is a measure of the **force of gravity** acting on an **object's mass**, pulling it toward the center of Earth. We measure this force when we place an object on a scale.

The force of gravity is nearly the same everywhere on Earth, so weighing an object tells us its mass.

In the U.S., the customary unit of measurement of mass is the pound (lb). The metric unit of measurement of mass is the kilogram (kg).

The blue whale's tongue weighs as much as an elephant, and its heart weighs as much as a car.

Olympic Weight Lifting

Olympic weight lifters compete by lifting weights above their heads. The weights are measured in kilograms. They are attached to a steel bar called a **barbell**. Equal sets of weights, called **plates**, are attached at either end of the barbell and secured in place with a **collar**. As the competition progresses, more weight is added. Weight increases by at least 1 kg (about 2.2 pounds) at a time. The weights are as follows:

Barbell **20 kg**
Collars (one at each end) **2.5 kg**
Plates: Large
Green **10 kg**
Yellow **15 kg**
Blue **20kg**
Red **25 kg**

Plates: Small
White **0.5 kg**
Green **1 kg**
Yellow **1.5 kg**
Blue **2 kg**
Red **2.5 kg**

This lifter has lifted the following weights:

Barbell (20 kg) + 2 x Collars (2 x 2.5 kg) + 2 x Large Red (2 x 25 kg) + 2 x Large Green (2 x 10 kg) + 2 x Small Yellow (2 x 1.5 kg)
= 98 kg

Weighing a Ton

One ton equals 196,000 pounds. The heaviest animal in the world, the blue whale, weighs **220 tons**. That's the weight of

2,500 adult humans.

The lightest mammal is the Etruscan shrew. It weighs just **0.003 pound**. One blue whale weighs more than

100 million Etruscan shrews.

Etruscan shrew

Temperature

Temperature is measured using scales that are based on the freezing and boiling points of water. The most common scale used around the world is Celsius, but the Fahrenheit scale is also used. The boiling point of water is 100°C (212°F). Its freezing point is 0°C (32°F).

Converting

These are the formulas for converting between Celsius and Fahrenheit:

$$°F = (°C \times {}^9/_5) + 32$$
$$°C = (°F - 32) \times {}^5/_9$$

Absolute Zero

An object's temperature is produced by the movement of atoms. The more rapidly the atoms move, the hotter the object becomes.

The temperature at which atoms would not move at all is known as **absolute zero**. This is a temperature of

-273.15°C

In Fahrenheit, that's -459.67°F! It is also defined as 0 Kelvin (0 K). 1 K equals absolute zero plus 1°C. Scientists believe that it is not possible to cool anything to 0 K, but they have managed to reach temperatures of less than **1 billionth of a Kelvin**.

Normal body temperature can range from

96.7°F (36.1°C)
to ## 98.7°F (37.2°C).

If we become much colder or warmer, that means we are sick.

"Brrr...it's a bit nippy up here!"

The temperature in open space is a chilly 2.7 K. That's

-454.81°F

(-270.45°C)

Moon Temperatures

The moon has no atmosphere to protect it, and so the temperature drops to -302°F (-150°C) at night but soars to about 248°F (120°C) during the day—literally boiling hot! Each time humans have landed on the moon, the landing has been timed to happen just after the lunar dawn, before the surface has become too hot.

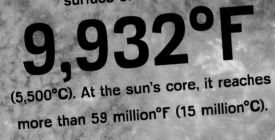

The temperature on the surface of the sun is

9,932°F

(5,500°C). At the sun's core, it reaches more than 59 million°F (15 million°C).

Telling the Time

A year is based on the time it takes Earth to complete an orbit of the sun. **A day** is the time it takes for Earth to turn once completely on its axis.

Months are roughly equal to the time it takes the moon to orbit Earth.

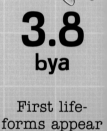

A sundial was an early clock that measured the time by showing the angle of the shadow of the sun. It can only work when the sun is shining.

We use a mix of measures to mark the passing of time. They are based on patterns our ancestors noticed in the changes of seasons, day, and night.

Dividing the Day

The ancient Greeks divided the daytime into 12 equal hours. As the amount of daylight varied through the year, the length of an hour varied—longer in summer and shorter in winter. The idea of dividing the whole day into 24 equal hours, also covering nighttime, was first proposed by the Greek astronomer Hipparcus in the second century BC, and this is the system we still use today.

13.7 bya	13.4 bya	5 bya	4.5 bya	3.8 bya
The universe starts with the Big Bang.	First galaxies start to form.	The sun forms.	Earth forms.	First life-forms appear on Earth.

Dividing the Hours

Hours are divided into **60 minutes**. **Minutes** are then divided into **60 seconds**. This system dates from the ancient Babylonians, who chose the number 60 because it can be **divided exactly** by lots of different numbers: **2, 3, 4, 5, 6, 10, 12, 15, 20, and 30**.

Counting the Years

As we add up the years, we do so in **multiples of 10**. A **decade** is 10 years. A **century** is 100 years. And a **millennium** is 1,000 years.

When talking about time on the scale of the history of the universe, scientists often talk of **mya**, which stands for "millions of years ago," and **bya**, which stands for "billions of years ago."

February
29

Leap Years

Most years are **365 days long**. But the time it takes for the sun to return to the same place in the sky each year is actually 365.24 days. To make a correction, every four years an extra day is added to make a leap year. However, this makes an average of **365.25 days**, which is a little too long, so 3 times every 400 years, a leap year is skipped.

A year is a leap year if:
Either it is divisible by 400, or it is divisible by 4 but not divisible by 100.

540 mya

First animals appear.

250 mya

First dinosaurs appear.

65 mya

Dinosaurs disappear.

200,000 years ago

First humans appear.

What Are We Measuring?

Measurements can give different answers depending on what you use to make the measurement and where you make it.

Losing Weight

"Where are the scales?"

The weight of an object varies depending on where you are weighing it. The farther away from the center of Earth you go, the weaker the force of gravity is. This means you would lose weight by climbing mountains, but only a little! At the top of Mount Everest, climbers weigh about 0.25 percent less than they do at sea level.

Walking on the Moon

The difference in weight would be much more dramatic if you traveled to the moon. A human who weighs **180 lbs on Earth** would weigh **just 30 lbs** on the surface of the moon. That's $\frac{1}{6}$ the weight. Because of the weaker gravity, astronauts on the moon had to be careful when walking around. If they tried to walk like we do on Earth, they would fly up into the air.

How Long Is the Coastline of an Island?

The length of a wiggly line will vary depending on the means of measurement you are using. Imagine you are measuring the line with a ruler. A short ruler will provide a larger answer than if a larger ruler is used because a shorter ruler is able to follow more of the wiggles of the coastline.

Measuring the coastline of Great Britain using lines of **62 miles** gives a length of

1,740 miles.

With lines of **31 miles**, it is

2,112 miles,

372 miles longer. If you walk the whole coast, using lines one pace (about 1 yard) long, it will be much longer still—about

11,184 miles.

So how long, exactly, is the coastline of Great Britain?

It all depends on how you measure it.

A metal tape measure can only measure objects in straight lines.

Exabyte
1,024 petabytes
Petabyte
1,024 terabytes
Terabyte
1,024 gigabytes
Gigabyte
1,024 megabytes
Megabyte
1,024 kilobytes
Kilobyte
1,024 bytes

How **Fast** Is Your **Computer?**

The smallest unit in a computer's memory is the bit. This can have one of two values: either "on" or "off" ("0" or "1"). Bits are arranged into groups of eight, called bytes. Individual pieces of information are stored on bytes, which form the "words" of the memory. For example:

01101001

11011110

Each bit in a byte can take one of two values. This means that the total different values a byte can take is

2 x 2 x 2 x 2 x 2 x 2 x 2 x 2 = 256

Computer memory, called the hard drive, has grown in size tremendously since the earliest computers. Modern computers have enormous numbers of bytes in their memory.

1956
The IBM 305 RAMAC had a memory of about 5 megabytes.

1984
The first Apple Macintosh computer had a memory of 128 kilobytes.

2012
The supercomputer Titan has a memory of 700 terabytes.

2015
A modern smartphone has about 16 gigabytes of memory.

Hands On

The Chinese supercomputer **Tianhe-2** can perform 34 quadrillion operations in one second. That's 34,000,000,000,000,000 operations! If every human on Earth performed one calculation per second, it would take more than a year to perform as many calculations as Tianhe-2 performs in a second.

Computer Speed

With such huge memories, computers need to work very quickly. The processing speed of modern home computers is measured in gigahertz (GH).

1 gigahertz is equal to 1 billion operations per second.

The Chinese supercomputer **Tianhe-2** can perform **34 quadrillion operations in one second**. That's **34,000,000,000,000,000** operations!

"Hold on, wait a second!"

"A jiffy is quicker!"

A Jiffy

Computers have interna[l] clocks that time their operatio[ns]. One click on a computer's clock is ca[lled] a "jiffy."

1 jiffy = about 10 ms (10 milliseconds).

Quiz

31 million miles

1 After the moon, the brightest object in the night sky is the planet **Venus**. At its closest to **Earth**, Venus is about

31 million miles away. If light takes **8 minutes** to reach us from the sun, **how long does light take to reach us** from Venus?

2 **How many liters** of water would it take to half-fill a cube-shaped box with sides **20 cm long?**

3 You see a bolt of lightning and count **10 seconds** before **hearing the thunder. How far away** was the lightning?

4 a) Running at a steady speed of **25 m/s**, **how long would it take** a cheetah to complete a **100 m** race?

10 SECONDS

b) If a man running at

10 m/s starts

the race **even** with the cheetah, **how far behind** will the man be when the cheetah **crosses the line**?

5 How much **weight** have these weight lifters lifted? **Hint:** *Look back at page 19 for the weights of the different colors. Don't forget the weights of the barbell and the collars.*

a) Barbell, collars, 2 red large, 2 green large, 2 blue small

b) Barbell, collars, 4 yellow large

c) Barbell, collars, 2 blue large, 2 red small, 2 white small

6 When astronaut Neil Armstrong landed on the moon, he was wearing a space suit that weighed

180 lbs on Earth.

Armstrong himself weighed **176 lbs**. Remembering that the moon has $\frac{1}{6}$ the gravity of Earth, how much did Armstrong in his space suit weigh on the moon?

7 a) Convert these temperatures to degrees **Fahrenheit**:

a) **15°C**

b) **-5°C**

c) **100°C**

8 Convert these temperatures to degrees **Celsius**:

a) **32°F**

b) **104°F**

c) **-40°F**

9 a) Venus is the hottest planet in the solar system, with an average surface temperature of

735 Kelvin.

How much is this in degrees Celsius (to the nearest whole degree)?

b) The average temperature on Earth is 14°C. **How many degrees Celsius** hotter is Venus than Earth?

F   C

120 — 50

100 — 40

80 — 30

60 — 20

40 — 10

20 — 0

0 — -10

-20 — -20

-40 — -30

-40

10 Which of the following years is not a leap year?

a) **2000**

b) **2032**

c) **2100**

11 Your new computer has a processing speed of

2.8 gigahertz.

How many operations can it perform in **10 seconds**?

12 The 1984 Apple Macintosh computer had

128 kilobytes

of memory. A certain new smartphone has **12.8 gigabytes** of memory. How many times as much memory does the phone have as the Apple computer?

Hint: *First convert the phone's memory into kilobytes. (There are approximately 1 million kilobytes in a gigabyte.) Use this value.*

Glossary

Acceleration
A change in an object's velocity, caused by applying a force. Acceleration can change the object's speed, the direction in which it is moving, or both.

Byte
The basic unit in a computer's memory. One byte is made of eight bits, each of which can take the value 0 or 1. A byte can take 256 different values.

Gigahertz
A measure of frequency equal to 1 billion cycles per second.

Gravity
A force that pulls bodies with mass toward one another. The larger a body's mass, the greater its pull.

Imperial
A system of measurement that was standardized across the British Empire in the 19th century. Many of the measurements are related to the body, such as the inch, foot, and yard.

Kelvin
A measure of temperature. 0 Kelvin (0 K), also known as absolute zero, is the minimum possible temperature. 0 K = -454.81°F (-273.15°C)

Leap year
A year that is 366 days long, one day longer than non-leap years. The extra day keeps years in line with Earth's orbit around the sun.

Light-year
A unit of length equal to the distance traveled by light in one year. Light travels at a speed of 186,272 miles per second, which means that in a year it travels 5.87 trillion miles.

Mass
A measure of the amount of matter contained in an object.

Metric
A standard system of measurement that uses units in multiples of ten. Also called the International System of Units, it contains three main units: meter, kilogram, and liter.

Nanotechnology
Engineering that takes place at the nanoscale, which is between 1 and a few hundred nanometers (billionths of a meter). At this scale, machines are built using individual molecules as their moving parts.

Velocity
A measure of an object's movement. Velocity is the speed of motion in a particular direction. Any change in speed or direction changes an object's velocity.

Weight
A measure of the force of gravity pulling any object toward Earth or another celestial body. The weight of an object is roughly the same wherever it is on Earth.

Index

Facts for Now

Visit this Scholastic Web site for more information
on measuring and to download the
Teaching Guide for this series:
www.factsfornow.scholastic.com
Enter the keywords **Get the Measure**

Answers

1. The sun is 93 million miles away. This is three times the distance of Venus, so the light from Venus takes $^8/_3$ minutes to reach us = 2 minutes 40 seconds.

2. The volume of the box is $20 \times 20 \times 20$ = 8,000 cm³ = 8 liters. To half-fill the box, you will need 4 liters of water.

3. 2 miles

4. a) It would take 4 seconds. b) After 4 seconds, the man will have covered 40 m, so he will be 60 m behind.

5. a) 99 kg b) 85 kg c) 71 kg

6. Total weight on Earth = 356 lbs. $356 \div 6 = 59$ lbs

7. a) 59°F b) 23°F c) 212°F

8. a) 0°C b) 40°C c) -40°C

9. a) $735 - 273 = 462$°C
b) Venus is 448°C hotter than Earth.

10. c) 2100 is not a leap year. It is divisible by 100 but not divisible by 400.

11. It performs 2.8 billion operations in one second, so in 10 seconds, it will perform 28 billion operations.

12. There are 1 million kilobytes in 1 gigabyte, so the phone has 12.8 million kilobytes of memory. $12.8 \text{ million} \div 128 = 100,000$